One Nation, One People

Judi Laman
Art by Joe Flood

Literacy Consultants
David Booth • Kathleen Corrigan

Contents

Preface 3

Chapter 1
A Historical Family Dinner 4

Chapter 2
Life, Liberty, and the
Pursuit of Happiness 8

Chapter 3
The Beginnings of Change 16

Chapter 4
Making Change a Reality 20

Chapter 5
Bringing the Past
Into the Present 27

Preface

President Lyndon Johnson was the thirty-sixth President of the United States, serving from 1963 to 1969. During that time, Johnson was a great advocate for the Civil Rights movement, accessibility to education and the arts, and urban and rural development. The changes he made during his presidency allowed many families to move away from poverty. His policies also provided federal funding for children of lower income families to continue their studies. Johnson worked to put an end to discrimination and segregation in public institutions, such as schools, promoting a more inclusive atmosphere for people of all backgrounds and races.

Chapter 1

A Historical Family Dinner

Miguel's home in San Antonio, Texas

It was Sunday afternoon, and Miguel's family was gathered around the dining room table for a big lunch to celebrate *bisabuela* Isabel's ninety-fifth birthday. They were having *huaraches*, so the table was filled with different kinds of food: the masa flatbread onto which all the ingredients would be piled; both green and red salsa; onions and beans; beef and chicken; and — Miguel's top choice for toppings — hot chilies. It was a feast, and huaraches were Miguel's favorite meal.

Miguel usually loved these family gatherings. The food was always delicious and the company lots of fun; there was plenty of laughter and stories to go around the table. His grandfather, *abuelo* Eduardo, also typically gave Miguel the coins from his pocket as a treat, which usually made him feel special. But today, Miguel wasn't in the mood for a big family meal, and he was more reserved than usual at the table.

"Miguel," his great-grandmother said, watching him intently, "why are you so quiet today?"

"I'm sorry, bisabuela," Miguel replied slowly. "I'm thinking about school, and how I don't want to go back tomorrow, and I wish I could just quit. Why do I need to go to school anyway?"

"Hey," Miguel's mother piped in, "what's this all about, son? What's troubling you?"

"I just don't want to go to school anymore," Miguel said. "I have a history project due tomorrow and, well, it's all so boring."

"Ah," Miguel's dad said, "it's a homework problem, is it?"

"It's not just that!" Miguel replied defensively. "I don't belong there, and none of the kids in my class are like me."

"What makes you say that?" Miguel's dad asked.

"We're completely different, *papá*! We don't have similar traditions or experiences, and even the food I eat isn't the same as what the other kids eat. Nobody brings this kind of stuff for lunch," he said, indicating the spread of authentic cuisine on the table, his eyes downcast. "I don't belong there."

"*Mi niño*," Miguel's mother said, embracing her son. "I didn't know you were having such a hard time. But believe me, you do belong there."

"Let me tell you a story," Isabel interjected softly. "It happened decades ago when I was just a girl. I had the good fortune to have Lyndon B. Johnson, the thirty-sixth President of the United States, as my schoolteacher."

"You had the President of the United States for a teacher?" Miguel gasped.

"Well," Isabel said with a chuckle, "he wasn't the President yet. The year was 1929 — "

Chapter 2

Life, Liberty, and the Pursuit of Happiness

Welhausen Elementary School in Cotulla, Texas
1929

Santiago put his hand high in the air. "The answer is forty-two," he said when his teacher, Mr. Johnson, called upon him.

"That's correct, Santiago."

Santiago smiled happily. His classmates and his friends around him nodded encouragingly. Mr. Johnson had been at the school since September, and all of his students loved him.

"You have come a long way, class, and I'm very proud of you all," Mr. Johnson told his students.

A young girl raised her hand. "Yes, Isabel, what is it?" asked Mr. Johnson.

"Well, Sir, I still don't understand why we need to learn all of this or where we might use this knowledge. My mother says this is the last year for me to go to school and that I'm going to be working in the fields with my brothers soon, so when will I put these lessons to use?"

Mr. Johnson frowned slightly. "Yes, I understand how that could leave you feeling that this isn't worth your time, but the only limit on what you do with your life comes from within. The more you learn and the more you push yourself, the more opportunities there can be for you."

"That might be true for you, Sir," Isabel broke in, "but it's not true for us. We can't afford to keep going to school, and the money my parents make is barely enough to get our family by as it is. That's why I'm going to end up working in the fields with the rest of my family after this school year so that I can contribute to the family income."

Mr. Johnson looked around at his students, who were nodding their heads in agreement.

"This is the United States of America, Isabel," Mr. Johnson explained, his brow furrowed. "Every man and woman has the ability to be whoever they want to be."

"No, Mr. Johnson," said Santiago, "that's your country, but our country is different because we don't have the same opportunities as you, and nobody cares if we spend our whole lives out in the fields."

"It was true," Miguel's great-grandmother said. "We all lived with our families in small, crowded shacks. My parents and older siblings spent their days from dawn to dusk hunched over in the fields, pulling weeds and harvesting crops. We were proud of the work we did. It was honest work, but it was hard — and it was the only work available to us. We had no influence in the community. We lived and worked there, but we were practically invisible."

"So what happened, bisabuela?" Miguel asked, completely immersed in his great-grandmother's intriguing story.

"Oh, well, our teacher, Mr. Johnson, wasn't about to let us give up without a fight," Isabel replied.

"We are one nation and one people," Mr. Johnson insisted. "Our fate as a nation and our future as a people rest not upon one citizen but upon all citizens, and in the United States — everybody counts."

"But some seem to count more than others!" a young boy from the back of the room dared to add; again, there were nods and mumblings of agreement from the students.

"Well," Mr. Johnson said, "how are we going to change that? What are we going to do to ensure that the United States that is available to me is also attainable for all of you — and for everyone in the country? How are we going to ensure that your voices are heard?"

There was some murmuring from the classroom, but none of the students raised their hands with any ideas.

"Listen," Mr. Johnson continued, "I know your situation is different from mine, but it shouldn't be, and it doesn't have to be. This country was built by people who shared the belief that every man and woman has the right to live as each one sees fit." He paced at the front of the room, scanning the faces of the innocent kids looking up at him. "We've talked about the Declaration of Independence, and right in that document it says, 'We hold these truths to be self-evident, that all men are created equal, that they are endowed by their Creator with certain unalienable Rights, that among these are Life, Liberty, and the pursuit of Happiness.'"

"You're right, sir," said Santiago. "But those are just some words on a sheet of paper, and that's not the way life really is for us because not everyone lives out those principles. Words are not enough to make change happen."

"Santiago was right. Words aren't enough, bisabuela," said Miguel. "People need to believe them, to follow them and demonstrate what the words mean. But people don't always do that."

"That's true," said bisabuela Isabel. "In fact, when I was a young girl, there were entire groups of people like us who were left on the outside looking in at a country we weren't necessarily a part of. Sure, we were Americans, and our family had resided in Texas since before it was a state, but we still didn't really have the same rights as Mr. Johnson did."

"So then he was wrong," Miguel surmised.

"No," his bisabuela disagreed. "Mr. Johnson was right, but we didn't see it just yet. People weren't living the way the laws had intended, but that didn't mean we couldn't abolish unfair practices, and Mr. Johnson was certainly up to the challenge."

Chapter 3

The Beginnings of Change

Welhausen Elementary School in Cotulla, Texas
1929

"So again I ask you, what are we to do?"
Mr. Johnson said, addressing his students.

Santiago raised his hand tentatively, and
Mr. Johnson nodded for him to speak.

"Well," Santiago began, "it seems that we have
rules that everyone is supposed to follow, but maybe
the rules aren't completely clear, and so people don't
always abide by them. So I guess you need someone to
make sure everyone respects the rules."

"You're right, Santiago," Mr. Johnson said. "We do
have the rules in place, but perhaps they aren't
always clear, and so they need to be fixed. Who do

you think should regulate the rules and make sure they're followed?"

The students were silent. Isabel raised her hand hesitantly. "The government, sir," she replied. "The government makes the rules for the country and makes sure that people follow them. The government can change the rules if they don't think they are effective enough or if they need to be more clear."

"That's right, Isabel. Can you share an example of when the government has modified laws that maybe weren't entirely productive? Perhaps something we have talked about in class?"

Isabel paused for a moment, thinking back to her lessons, and then replied, "Women's rights. The government fixed the laws to make sure that women would have the right to vote, just the same as men."

"That's right, Isabel! Remember, class, before the Nineteenth Amendment was passed, there were still many places in the United States where women's rights were not equal to men's rights, and they couldn't vote."

Santiago raised his hand. "That was when Susan B. Anthony and Elizabeth Cady Stanton started organizing a group to stand up for women's rights."

"Exactly, Santiago, and it didn't happen right away. They first established the National Woman Suffrage Association in 1869 to work toward those rights, but the Nineteenth Amendment wasn't ratified until 1920. It took more than fifty years for women to attain the same rights that men had always enjoyed. But there were lots of positive developments happening at that time and many people working hard to bring about transformation in all kinds of ways."

The class was humming with excitement now. Students' faces lit up as they thought about changes they might like to see implemented.

"So if we want to see change," Santiago concluded, glancing around at his nodding classmates, "we need to start working now to make it happen."

Chapter 4

Making Change a Reality

Miguel's home in San Antonio, Texas

"Of course, it still wasn't easy," Isabel said to Miguel and the family sitting around the table, all eyes on her as she continued with her story. "I did end up working in the fields with my brothers the next year, but I never forgot Mr. Johnson — and he didn't forget us either."

"What do you mean?" Miguel asked.

"Well, it seems that he wasn't just throwing words about in our classroom. He believed them with his heart, but just as with the shift in women's rights, it took time to influence change. He never stopped working for it, though."

"So what happened next? Do you remember, abuelo?" Miguel asked.

"Your bisabuela would never let me forget," Miguel's grandfather chimed in, looking at his mother with a small smile. "Mr. Johnson didn't stay a schoolteacher: he decided to serve in government. By the time I was a few years older than you are now, he was quite accomplished and had worked his way up to one of the highest jobs in government. He then took over the U.S. presidency in 1963, and we were lucky that he was passionate about the rights of Americans. In fact, in 1964, he signed the Civil Rights Act into law, and it revolutionized the United States."

"Really?" Miguel asked, completely intrigued now. "What did it say?"

"Hang on, I think I have a history book here somewhere with the speech," Miguel's mother said, getting up from the table. A few minutes later she returned with an old textbook and turned to a page. "Here it is," she said, consulting the book and clearing her throat to read a passage. "This is part of the speech in which he addressed the nation in Washington on July 2, 1964." She began to read.

" 'Americans of every race and color have worked to build a nation of widening opportunities. Now our generation of Americans has been called on to continue the unending search for justice within our own borders. We believe that all men are created equal. Yet many are denied equal treatment. We believe that all men have certain unalienable rights. Yet many Americans do not enjoy those rights. We believe that all men are entitled to the blessings of liberty. Yet millions are being deprived of those blessings — not because of their own failures, but because of the color of their skin. The reasons are deeply imbedded in history and tradition and the nature of man. We can understand — without rancor or hatred — how this all happened. But it cannot continue. Our Constitution, the foundation of our Republic, forbids it. The principles of our freedom forbid it. Morality forbids it. And the law I will sign tonight forbids it.' "

Miguel's mother paused to scan her son's face. Then she continued, "This line of his speech was perhaps the crux of everything he fought for: 'Let us lay aside irrelevant differences and make our Nation whole.'"

"So did that make things better, abuelo?" Miguel asked.

"It was a start," answered abuelo Eduardo, "and it certainly got things headed in the right direction. It's certainly why you go to school now with kids from lots of different backgrounds: the Act made schools and other institutions more inclusive. But even that wasn't good enough for President Johnson. So he persevered, forever wanting to fulfill his vision of something he called 'A Great Society.'"

"What's that?" Miguel asked.

"It was President Johnson's set of ideas for fixing things like poverty, education, health care, and civil rights. He wanted to make a real difference in the lives of all Americans, people like — "

"People like bisabuela!" Miguel interrupted.

"Exactly!" Isabel confirmed. "He worked hard to give all Americans the same rights. Mr. Johnson was passionate about education, and he wanted everyone to have equal opportunity. The government established laws and made money available to build more schools, and they provided students with the money to attend those schools. That gave people the option to continue with school so that they could choose to keep learning and training for better-paying jobs."

Isabel paused for a few seconds, reminiscing about the day that still made her smile with pride. "I remember hearing President Johnson speak after he signed the Higher Education Act in 1965. He said he always remembered my class. We'd helped him see that not everyone has the option to go to college or to continue their education. He said that it was then, in my classroom, that he made up his mind that he wouldn't rest until the door to knowledge was open for all citizens."

"You and your classmates did influence change after all, bisabuela," Miguel chimed in with pride.

"That new law made it possible for me to continue to go to school," abuelo Eduardo added. "I was the first in our family to go to college, and I wouldn't have been able to do it without the funding that President Johnson helped create."

Chapter 5

Bringing the Past Into the Present

Miguel considered what his abuelo and his bisabuela had told him about how far things had come for them, but he was still conflicted. "I understand how all of this feels important to you, since both of you were directly affected by it," Miguel said, "but I'm not sure it really has much to do with me not fitting in at school."

"Oh, it does, *mi niño*, it does," abuelo Eduardo replied. "You see, the chances you have today weren't always there for our family. You heard what your bisabuela said about not being able to afford to go to school. I remember her working in those fields when I was a boy. My mother is one of the brightest people I have ever known, but she didn't have the opportunities that I did — and you have even more opportunities than I had. If your bisabuela had had the option, she would have continued with her studies. You do have that option, so you can't take your education for granted."

"But still," Miguel persisted, "I'm nothing like the other kids in my class."

"Honey," Miguel's mother said, "pass me a masa."

Miguel did as his mother asked and passed one of the flatbreads over to her. Miguel's mother laid the masa on the plate and began spooning things onto it.

"Now," she said, "there are lots of different things I can put on my masa, right?"

Miguel looked at all of the food on the table. "Well yes, *mamá*, of course. Look at all the different toppings we can choose from!"

Miguel's mother spread some green salsa on the masa, then she piled on some beans and onions, and finally she added a little bit of chicken.

"So," she said, sweeping her hand over her plate, "is this a huarache?"

Miguel laughed. "Well, of course it is, mamá," he said. "But it's not the way I would eat it because I like red salsa, beef, and hot chilies on it!"

"That's right," Miguel's mother said. "But everyone has different tastes. That's why we have so many different things on the table to go onto the masa. But no matter what you choose to put on it, you are still making a huarache, right?"

Miguel nodded in agreement.

"Your mamá is a clever woman," bisabuela Isabel continued. "Her huarache has lots of different ingredients to give different flavors. There are so many options to put on the masa, but in the end, they all end up as huaraches. It is the same with the United States: people come from many different cultural backgrounds, and we all have different customs, and even different foods! But that brings a variety of understandings and views, and that difference is good for the country."

"So what you're saying is that it is OK to be different from the other kids at school because we're all a little bit different in our own way?"

Isabel clapped her hands and gave a little hoot of approval, and everyone laughed.

"Miguel," abuelo Eduardo said, "do you have one of those coins I gave you earlier?"

Miguel fished a quarter out of his pocket and showed it to his grandfather.

"Does it have an eagle on one side?" As Miguel nodded, abuelo Eduardo continued, "Somewhere there with the eagle are the words *E pluribus unum*. That is Latin, and I don't suppose you know what that means, do you?"

Miguel shook his head and his abuelo Eduardo explained, "It means 'Out of many, one.' It is a motto for our country, since the United States is made up of many states that all banded together to form one country. Do you see?"

"Yes," Miguel said. "I didn't think of it before, but that's what the name means."

"We are also a land made up of many people who have all come together as Americans," his abuelo continued. "Your family history may be different from that of the other students, but you are still an American. We have differences, but together we are one."

"Just like the huaraches," Miguel said with a laugh.

"Yes, just like the huaraches," Miguel's mother agreed with an approving smile.

"So what are we going to do about your history project?" Miguel's father asked.

"Well, I think I'd like to talk about President Johnson and how he helped people with education — that is, if everyone here can give me a hand with it," Miguel said, looking around at his family.

"That sounds splendid," said Isabel. "But first, let's eat our huaraches!"